A Wheel in a Wheel

A Wheel in a Wheel

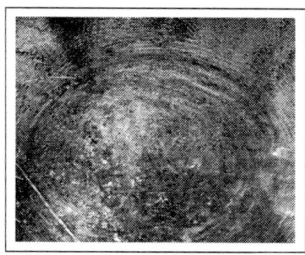

Poems by

Gretchen Schafer Skelley

Antrim House
Simsbury, Connecticut

Copyright © 2011 by Gretchen Schafer Skelley

Except for short selections reprinted for purposes of
book review, all reproduction rights are reserved.
Requests for permission to replicate should
be addressed to the publisher.

ISBN: 978-0-9843418-9-4

Printed & bound by United Graphics, Inc.

First Edition, 2011

Front cover photograph by Rennie McQuilkin

Book design by Rennie McQuilkin

Antrim House
860.217.0023
AntrimHouse@comcast.net
www.AntrimHouseBooks.com
21 Goodrich Road, Simsbury, CT 06070

To my father, the Rev. Walter Schafer,
a gentle spirit in a loving man

Thanks to Polly Zarella, who first thought of a book; to Lucy Townsend, who gave me a publisher, Antrim House; to Rennie McQuilkin for his guidance and his knowledge; and to Kathleen McGrory, critic and friend par excellence.

Table of Contents

PROEM

Spider / 3

I. ELEMENTS

On the Litchfield Road / 7
Tibi II / 8
Haiku / 9
For Joan / 10
Dry Spell / 11
For My Father / 12
Pentecost / 13

II. LOVE'S MEASURE

Ransom / 17
The Acrobat on Balance / 18
Centripetal Force / 21

ABOUT THE AUTHOR / 23

...as if a wheel had been in the midst of a wheel.

Ezekiel X: 10

*The big wheel run by faith an'
the little wheel run by the grace o' God:
a wheel in a wheel:
' way in the middle of the air.*

traditional spiritual

Proem

Spider

Deliberately, in the dim, silent room she
places each fragile thread drawn from her
own body with what dull resignation
no human can describe.

The pattern – eons old – is set. No random
eccentricity betrays her. No witness points
and shouts

> *Here*
> *Arachne*
> *weaves*
> *who*
> *won the*
> *wrath of*
> *grey-eyed*
> *grim*
> *Athena*
> *(jealous of*
> *her skill)*
> *and –*
> *merely*
> *mortal –*
> *hung*
> *herself*
> *with a*
> *thick*
> *rope!*

I, knitting, tell myself that
God works to a larger pattern.
But warned tonight of that poor spinner
caught in the icy web of her perfection,
I hesitate – then stop – and   a stitch.
                      drop

I. Elements

On the Litchfield Road

Come, let's play on the mountain:
    slide down the hot, bright bolt
    of the bird's song
    through the cool
    green air and into the
river.

Brown rocks nudge us as we
    slip – all boneless – past
    trout languidly fanning
    themselves in place
    against the current.

Come, hide in this eddy!
    …and so we'll turn and dance.
    A twig pushes us over into
    the tumble and flash of white
water.

Cold muscles all compressed, at last
    we'll glide with water snakes
    along the gold-brown sand
    to feed and…
        dream…
            captive among the reeds.

Tibi II

Come and talk. Crush
Any tantalizing catnip and
Take catnaps any time,
        Companion
        And
        Tyrant.
                Oh
                    CAT.

Haiku

Cat in the window,
bluejay in the holly tree –
Mexican stand-off.

The fox knows many tricks,
the porcupine just one.
It's a good one.

For Joan

Joy or a new sorrow made your eyes snap,
oh Dandelion Girl. Your hair, pale filaments
all white and gold, you run some nights beside me.
Now water – gold and brown – enfolds us
and we swim together.

Joyless
on a narrow cot I've lain
and dreamt all
night of wind and laughter, Joan.

Dry Spell

What is it keeps me mute in my study?
Is it time or space I need?
Or the pure light of an August morning
washed on a keel by the sea?
Once those shadows on the fresh grass
painted my pictures for me or
the silver undersides of the
poplar leaves echoed the moon
and said, *Here it is! Take it!*
This is what light holds for you.
Dreaming is not enough!

For My Father

Within a lost time, remembering, we
attempt – lovingly – to enter rooms we always
left together, to walk along lost
trails, explore remoteness
      and – weary at last – return,
trudging, each of us waving a lost treasure.

    Thus
        endless
refreshment wells anew from loss –
      the eternal reservoir of God's good
          grace.

Pentecost

Dee! Dee! Dee! shrills the insistent bird –
You have been silent too long!

All memories confound us in the end.
Old love's cold meat – the sentimental fat
that clogs the lean of passion.

Old arts forsake us in the end.
Cold fingers warped by time cannot
command the waiting harp.

Old truths betray us in the end –
become blurred clearings in a wood
of lies in which we're lost again.

And what have we who slept like
children in that wood?
The worms usurp our bed.

Ideas rot beneath the weight of mold.
What is there then?

The eternal sun is there and water
and the bird's *Dee! Dee!*
that ushers in the spring.

Unless the leaf rots,
unless the worm works,
unless the bird cries,
no life will come.

Unmake me, Lord.
Dissolve me into elements again.
Define me with the worm,
the leaf,
the bird.

Belittle me to atoms.
Then begin.

II. Love's Measure

Ransom

Tell me, oh Time, how I may measure love.
How much have I to give, how much to save
safe for that heedless one who holds my heart
but will not give me his? I long to say,

"Then keep your heart but let each beat be mine.
I'll pile them up and count them, one by one,
a golden hoard to treasure with these jewels:
the rose you gave me and the ring I wear."

And when we two shall come to deal with Death,
I'll let them fall and shimmer at his feet.
Oh may he take this ransom for my love,
that you may live when all-consuming Death
has taken even that poor, empty box
that held my heart in hostage to your own.

The Acrobat on Balance

1.

Remember:
other people walk tightropes,
hands shaking,
ears pounding,
in tenuous balance
making it look easy.

2.

Climbing the ladder I feel with my fingers
for each reacquaintance with rope and with rigging
leading me up through the palpable darkness,
drawn by my reflexes onto the wire.

Over arenas I feel no distractions;
only my fingers and feet feel sensation.
Under my heart beats the pulse of the drummer,
light silvers my spine to the shimmer of cymbals.

Now when I see you, firm on your platform,
lifting your bar with one foot on the wire,
how I can dance then, heedless of catchers,
pointing my toes out, perfectly balanced…

"Bow to me, Partner. The act is beginning."

3.

Love, let us dance once again on the wire.
What do we care for their open-mouthed wonder?
Here where we run through the light and the shadow
only the wire – at last – understands us.

Quickly we venture out, testing the tension,
bowing together, formality hallowed;
ritual somersaults split us and join us.
Lovers, we dance out our joy on the wire.

4.

Balance ennobles us; our concentration
brings benediction if we can keep it.
Now I await you, bearing my burden
(each day more precious,
needing attention).

Oh, how our feet burn, dancing on wire.
Only the wire somehow sustains us;
only the wire now to connect us.
If we should falter
who, Love, could save us?

Now you approach me, carefully, slowly,
bearing your trio, The Triple Enchantment,
balanced in shimmer – smiling – above you.
See how their spangles glint in the darkness.

We – with our spines stretched –
we – with our palms wet –
feel for our footing.
Merciless spotlights.

Balance, Beloved! Balance –
I've lost it!

5.

The moment my foot slips, a wild
exhilaration fills me. A hard freeze
runs through all my muscles.
In full spangled splendor I fall and the
moment stretches as my feet stretch,
seeking the wire. My soul floats upward
over the tent pole, free of the canvas.
Free! How I welcome the chance
to be choiceless: welcome a racing toward
Death that is dreamless.
Sound is a scream drawn like
thread through a needle.
Faster and faster I fall.

Centripetal Force

For years she was the point round which you
swung in dizzying concentric circles –
the axis of your world,
the pivot of your top.
You sang
         and spun
                  and traveled.
She stayed at the calm center
                          still.

Now you've replaced her there. Though
she may
        swing
                  wider and more
    wildly yet
than ever you,

calmly you bring her home,
reeling her in like a kite on a line,
holding her fast in that still focused
love.

Gretchen Schafer Skelley was born and raised in Hartford, Connecticut. She was educated at the Chaffee School and Connecticut College for Women, where she was the first recipient of the Benjamin T. Marshall Prize for Poetry. While raising a family she was active in educational affairs, both in her daughters' school and at Chaffee. She was for some time a guide at Nook Farm, which comprises the homes of Harriet Beecher Stowe and Mark Twain. Her main occupation was as a teacher of Hatha Yoga at Hartford College for Women and in the Hartford and Simsbury areas. She now lives in West Hartford with her cat. She has always thought that poets should be young, tall and willowy. She is none of these things, but her cat loves her anyway.

This book is set in Garamond Premier Pro, which had its genesis in 1988 when type-designer Robert Slimbach visited the Plantin-Moretus Museum in Antwerp, Belgium, to study its collection of Claude Garamond's metal punches and typefaces. During the mid-fifteen hundreds, Garamond — a Parisian punch-cutter — produced a refined array of book types that combined an unprecedented degree of balance and elegance, for centuries standing as the pinnacle of beauty and practicality in type-founding. Slimbach has created an entirely new interpretation based on Garamond's designs and on comparable italics cut by Robert Granjon, Garamond's contemporary.

To order additional copies of this book
or other Antrim House titles, contact the publisher at

Antrim House
21 Goodrich Rd., Simsbury, CT 06070
860.217.0023, AntrimHouse@comcast.net
or the house website (www.AntrimHouseBooks.com).

•

On the house website
are sample poems, upcoming events,
and a "seminar room" featuring supplemental biography,
notes, images, poems, reviews, and
writing suggestions.